The WRANKERS

Erks, berks & Lumpy Jumpers!

BY DES BUCKLEY

The WRANKERS

Erks, berks & Lumpy Jumpers!

Authored & produced by Nelsons Eye Art Publications
'Lisafooka' 100 Broadstairs Road, Broadstairs, Kent CT10 2RU

Layout by Peter Cooke

Second edition published April 2018

The WRANKERS – the first 100 years!

THIS Cartoon compendium celebrates the 'invisible men and women of the Royal Air Force' the 'Wrankers.' They sit on the bottom rung of the RAF hierarchy and make up the majority of the workforce. Their contribution is easily overlooked in our understandable admiration for those magnificent men and women in their flying machines.

The monikers 'Erk, Berk & Lumpy jumpers' reflect the humour and quality of the Wranker. 'Erk,' references the cockney pronunciation of the word aircraft, 'Berk' is benign stupidity 'Lumpy Jumper' is an affectionate description of an RAF woolly 'pully' jumper on the female form.

A 'Wranker' is a 'junior rank' anything from a raw recruit to a Corporal. They are the RAF's equivalent of the Army 'squaddie' or the Navy's 'Matelot.' Even the humblest 'Wranker,' with a barely an opposable thumb, tends to consider themselves the intellectual superior of their Army and Navy siblings. The Wranker has evolved over 100 years. The men and women of 1918 could scarcely imagine the huge social and technological advances of today's RAF. From sail makers to drone operatives. Greater diversity and welfare developments have massively improved the lot of the ordinary Wranker. Today's RAF is a leaner service with more emphasis on individual performance and yet the character, spirit, fun, truculence and ability to keep going remain constant.

By far the greatest loss of life and limb in the RAF is overwhelmingly borne by our Aircrew. Post war conflicts however exact a cost on all personnel. Ground trades whilst generally less exposed to risks also take casualties & throw up people capable of acts of valour. Whilst recognising them all, this book focuses on our ordinary men & women. Their feet may be on the ground but some heads are in the clouds.

The time spent as a Wranker may be short or prolonged depending on branch or trade. The RAF employs legions of technical types some of whom ascend the ranks like a rocket. Other trades might take a fair while longer! The Wranker experiences their share of minor injustices and indignities. Try as it might the RAF cannot function without those in the support trades such as riggers, sooties, fairies, shineys, liney's, scab pickers, mouth miners, blanket stackers, snowdrops, rock apes, tags, oggies and the rest. This is not a learned academic study or an angry rant. It's an impossible task to represent every Wranker who laboured, skived, played, dawdled, innovated, flirted, endured, prospered, suffered, sacrificed and served. This is a genuinely affectionate ramshackle tribute and loud raspberry to Wrankers past and present wherever they may be. Bless them all, the long, the short and the tall…

WRANKER'S...
ROMANCE
..LOVES LABOURS LOST?...
Melodrama at the BOP
WILL SHE LOVE ME FOR MY MIND?
IT'S OVER!... I NEED MENTAL STIMULATION & FUN TO FULFILL ME....
I'VE GOT A COPY OF WRANKERS ERKS, BERKS & LUMPY JUMPERS...
HMMM HAS IT GOT LOTS OF PICTURES?
IF ONLY I DIDN'T LIVE IN A 10 MAN ROOM
YES & IT'S NOT STODGY IT'S GOT NO CHAPTERS & SUBJECTIVE CONTENT...
SOUNDS PROMISING BUT LOOKY THERE
I'M INTO SEWING & THAT GOOD LOOKING LAD HAS WAY MORE BADGES THAN YOU...
TATERS
RANDOM STUFF HISTORY, TRADES. BASIC TRAINING
CALL ME?
FOR HAPPIER ENDINGS→
PTO

Rejoice "in The Few"
but now Celebrate
the MANY the
Royal Air Force
"WRANKers!"....
COOOOOEEE
Near far where-ever...
COCKPIT
RAF GALLEON
DESMONDE

100 years of Marching ...
the Royal Air Force
Me Goat
"Baggy Trousers?"
"STOP this is MADNESS ... it's ...
....Screaming..
Lift.. Rite.. Lift.. Rite....."
erleft.. erright
.... Sweating
Spluttering..
desmondz

bimbling, Tik-Tocking, Limping...
..Ambling, Square Bashing, Whistling...
...Excellance
Ting-a-ling... ing..
ATG
STILL GOING Strong
desMONDE

WRANKERS CARRYING OFFICERS since Pontius Was a Pilot!

Lord Trenchard shows off his "WRANKER" Family
DESMONDE

The Royal Air Force
Influential men including WINSTON CHURCHILL & JAN SMUTS supported the FORMATION of the WORLDS 1st 'INDEPENDENT AIR Force
A third JUNIOR SERVICE ARRGGGH!
1st April 1918 the LAST YEAR of World WAR 1
GOOOOOE!
DESMONDE
The RAF allegedly set up at Cecil Hotel in the STRAND LONDON
A PLAQUE NOW MARKS the SPOT OF the RAF's First HQ

RUM, Sodomy & the LASH
Spit & Polish
Greese & Jodhpurs
BRAVE NEW WORLD?
RUM
ROYAL NAVY
"ROYAL NAVAL AIR SERVICE"
ARMY
(originally the ROYAL Engineers ...then)
→ RFC
ROYAL FLYING CORPS.
Established.
ROYAL AIR FORCE
1st APRIL 1918
In the Beginning...
THE FIRST & Largest Independent MILITARY AIRFORCE IN the WORLD
The BASTARD CHILD of the ARMY & NAVY!
the JUNIOR SERVICE
With Hotchpotch & "Handmedown" uniforms
desmonde

1920's
A financial Reckoning
The Policing of
Post WAR WORLD
We MUST REDUCE MILITARY SPending
Me again chaps the RAF could utilise Air & ground Assets to provide Cost Effective DEFENCE of MIDDLE EAST & other overseas Territories
The RAF MiniMises need for HUGE OVERSEAS GARRISONS - REPLACED BY AIRPOWER
& PRE-Regt ARMOURED CAR SQNS backed up by local LEVIES

Early Trades
Professional Doper
Recreational Doper
DESMONDE 2017.

AND FOR TODAY'S AIRFIELD MASS I'VE ASKED SISTER BRADY TO TAKE THE COLLECTION!

What do you Mean Sir has taken your Plimsoles?
RAF
DESMOND

Pioneering Air Land Ops
in defence of Empire
Oooops
Sausages?
BULLY BEEF
1
1
1
DROP ZONE SCORE
DESMONDE 2017

WOW LOOK at that GLORIOUS SUNSET
YOU DON'T That in NORRIS GREEN
OIH Noel COWARD SHINE the LIGHT HERE SUMMINK TICKLED Me JACKSIE!

Youth Education & Service Mythologys 1930's
GATHER ROUND LADS THIS IS THE TOMB OF THE "BAD APPRENTICE" NOTE THE POORLY FITTED PUTTEES
British Museum
Egyptian Rooms
Wilson
Keppel
Betts
"Ginger" Egyption Mummy
DESMONDE

I Fear McTAVISH MAY Not have the right TEMPREMENT for CONTROL ROOM Duty Sir
TAKE THAT YOU NAZI BASTARDS

LOOK HERE HQ I HAD A VACANCY FOR A "CHIRPY COCKNEY" & YOU'VE SENT a "BOLSHIE BRUMMIE!"
JESMONDE 2017

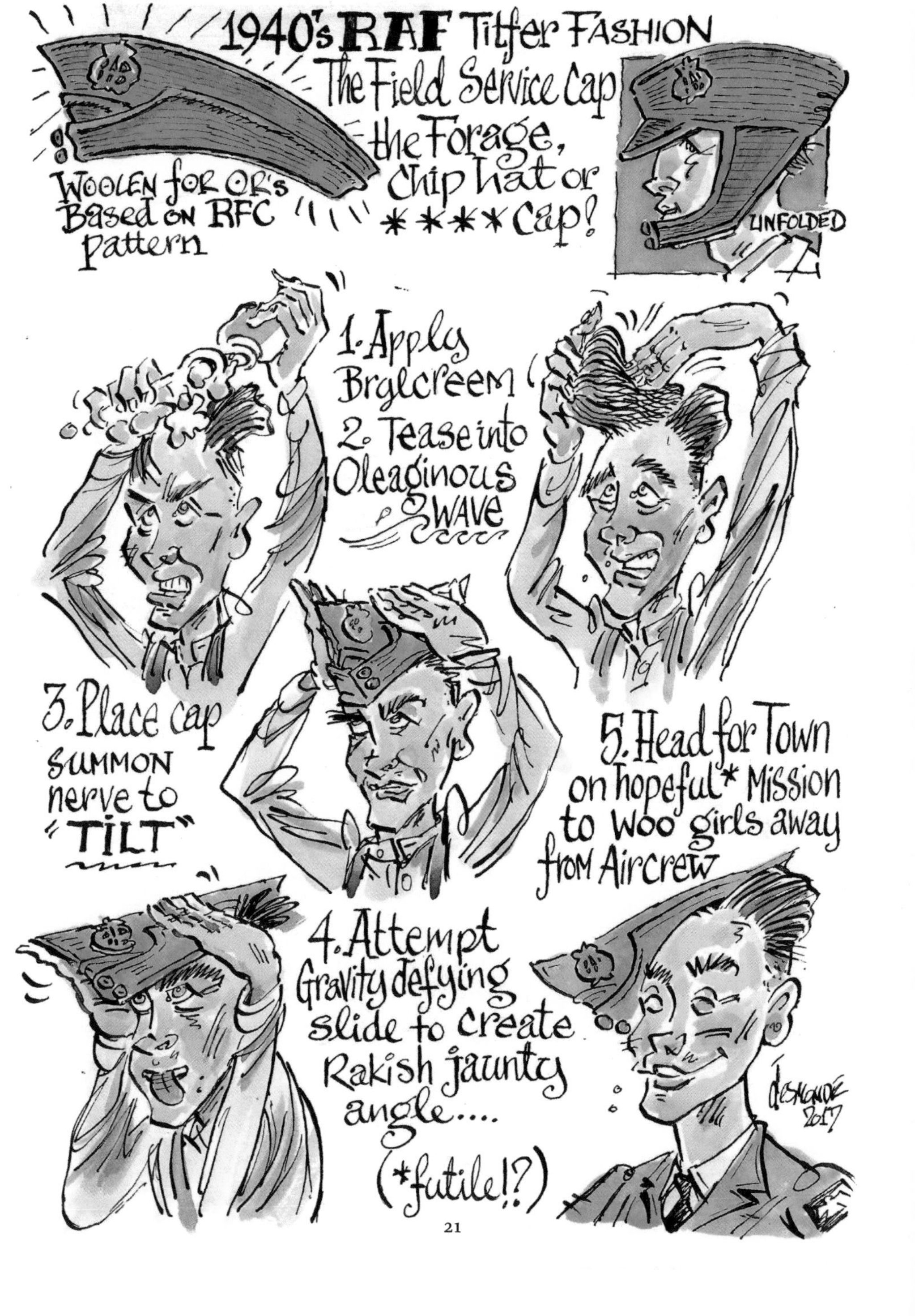

1940's RAF Titfer FASHION
The Field Service Cap
the Forage, Chip hat or ****Cap!
WOOLEN FOR OR's Based ON RFC pattern
UNFOLDED
1. Apply Brylcreem
2. Tease into Oleaginous WAVE
3. Place cap SUMMON nerve to "TILT"
5. Head for Town on hopeful* Mission to Woo girls away from Aircrew
4. Attempt Gravity defying slide to create Rakish jaunty angle....
(*futile!?)
DESMONDE 2017

Albert RN is Knocked out of the Stalag Luft XI Mannequin Cup by LAC Murphy RAF under the Noses of the Luftwaffe.

Duty Dentist!
DENTIST
DESMONDE

LOOK SKIP THE BLOODY GROUND CREW HAVE BEEN PLANTING TOMATOES IN the CAB AGAIN!
DESMONDE

OK CHAPS YOU CAN SHOOT AT THIS CHAPPY BUT NOT AT THE ANGRY LITTLE RAF CHAPS, THEY DON'T LIKE IT
desMONDE

The Whole of Lincolnshire to chose from & they Piss against our Wheels!
desMONDE

They'll be Bluebirds....
LOOK 'ERE VERA YOU SAID WHEN ALL THIS WAS OVER JIMMY COULD SLEEP IN HIS OWN LITTLE BED AGAIN!
JIMMY DOVER
Blighty
desmonde.

SICK PARADE to the MEDICAL CENTRE MARCH
LEFT, Groan, Limp, hobble, scream like a banshee, RIGHT!
OOOOOH
DAVID LANGDON
DESMONDE 2017

He's very Good
he's the Barrack Room Lawyer's
BARRACK ROOM LAWYER!
Psst

Hi Pop can you shave my Hairy Mary
DESMONDE

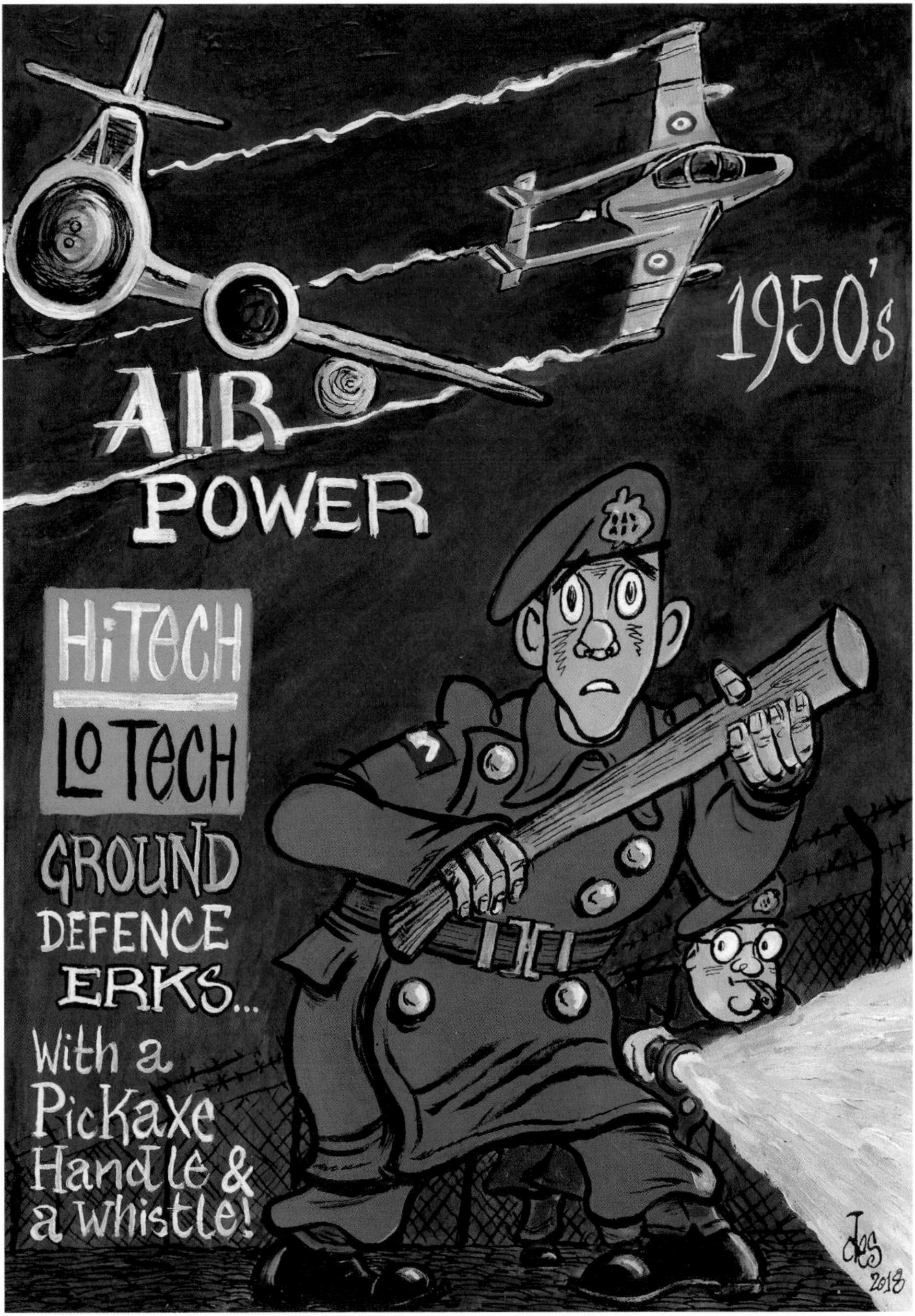
1950's
AIR POWER
HiTECH
LoTECH
GROUND DEFENCE ERKS...
With a PicKaxe Handle & a whistle!
Jes 2018

A Lift to the Mess
1940's

Lift to the Mess
2016
DESMONDE 2017

Basic Training
DESMONDE

BRASSO
INCOMING
DESMONDE 2017

BASIC TRAINING
The Identification of the Flight Shite Magnet

The awful Moment you Realise it's your turn to be the "SHIT MAGNET!"...
Miscreants without their Hi-Quality Towel Cravats.. FORWARD!
BACK
BACK
BACK
BACK
BACK
Desmond

Salute with your Right Hand you Muppets
Mascots
creatures demanding Respect
The descent of "recruit" Man?
DOGS
FLUFFY
ANGUS
desmonde

LISTEN UP LADS, YOUR REAL MILITARY TRAINING STARTS NOW. CORPORAL - BRING IN THE RECRUITS' LATEST HI-CALIBRE PERSONAL WEAPON...
RAF X71XD4 SHINE COMMANDO MANUAL 1953
Floor Polish Bumper
RAF

Something we Said?
MACBOLLOX!
DESMONDE
"DON'T CALL US CIVVY STREET REJECTS!" Thanks Pete!

THE ULTIMATE X FACTOR "Audition"
MARCH UP SALUTE STATE YOUR NAME RANK & NUMBER -- NOW
MARCH NOT Mince
C'MON LEFT RIGHT YOU FOOL
GET a MOVE ON WE'VE HOMES TO GO TO
HAHAHA
SO YOU THINK it's FUNNY to be an IDIOT?
over violent Salute!
TEHEHEE
Forgot your own NAME?
GRRRR
TAKE YOUR PAY TURN & GO...
des
New Recruits PAY PARADE Forget how to WALK & talk under the CRITICAL eyes of Instructors

Her Majesty could call on you to defend her- so on My order with Live rounds go..on..
REMEMBER Wot we tort you the Best get a BADGE!
Psst aim OFF or they will Post you to the RAF Regiment!
desmond 2018

I CAN'T WORK YOU OUT RUBIK
DESMONDE

Now then sunshine Never you mind them Hairyplanes the RAF has a more specialist Role for little old you!...
DESMONDE
Trades
Trades Selection National Service style!

OK chaps your Sgt & I spent hours matching your abilities to the most appropriate TRADE..... so from Left to Right ..."Wingnut"- RADAR, "Hawkeye"- MT, "Spotty"- Cook, McGowan- DENTAL tech, "Slugger"- ADMIN TYPIST, "Voldermort"- MED Asst & "Lofty"- RAF REGT... No questions, good...
FALL OUT!
PMO
VACANCIES
DESMONDE

Early beginnings - "One step forward"....
Despite the success of WW1 WRAF they were stood down after hostilities but reformed in 1939 as the WAAF

*T.E. LAWRENCE AKA 'LAWRENCE of Arabia', AKA. A.C. ROSS - AKA - A.C. SHAW RAF 1922-1935

WRAF, WAAF, RAF, PMRAFNS & RAuxAF....
"Sisters doing it for-
Themselves!"
1918-2018
des MONDE
2017

COPIES OF THIS POSTER AVAILABLE FROM 'WOMEN IN THE RAF 100' - TRISHIA WELSH *
CONTACT ME VIA MY WEBSITE FOR THEIR CONTACT DETAILS

AirWomen finding ways to JAZZ up unflattering
UNIFORMS since....... 1918
Sarge's gone
with acknowlegments to Fougasse
DESMONDE
2018.

Here Ablusions
WTF?
USE THESE IT KEEPS the SQUADDIES AMUSED & STOPS THEM MAKING RUDE COMMENTS WHEN YOU'RE IN THERE

..It's RAINING MEN.. Alleluia!....
It's MEDIC HUMOUR Sarge
deSMONDE

SHE INTIMIDates Me!
Ken
KEN
Boyfriend Material?
KEN
RAF Barbeee
RAF Combat Barbeee
RAF Combat Barbeee
Professor Lomski
Relationship Counsellor Model
DOLL DOG
With Free Pipe Vaper
desMONDE 2017

RAF
MILITARY COMIX
Romance
HE TOLD ME HE WAS A FLIGHT Engineer Not a Clerk with a Moped & a part time delivery JOB!
PIZZA
L
The Perils of Station BOP fantacists
HE COULD WRITE ACCURATE REPORTS BUT HE TALKED FICTION
desmonde 2018

RAF
desmonde

All New 1918 GROUND TRADES
ROYAL AIR FORCE NEW SERVICE
Coach Painter, VULCANISERS
WIREMAN, DOPER, CLERKS,
FABRIC WORKERS, SHOE Makers
Riveters Drivers CARPENTERS
NURSES
Wheelers Batman
Cook
BLACKSMITHS
Fitters · HOSPITAL ORERLYS
GENERAL DUTIES
MIX 'N MATCH UNIFORMS
MEN & WOMEN BUILD NEW SERVICE TOGETHER
IF YOU JOIN VOLUNTARILY YOU CANNOT BE Transfered To the ARMY OR NAVY WITHOUT YOUR CONSENT
2018 More ROLES than Greggs
GROUND TRADES
Inteligence Analyst · Avionics
Media · Flight OPs · Admin ·
RAF Regiment · Gen Mech
COMMS & Infrastruture ·
Survival EQUIPMENT TECH ·
Musician · CATERING ·
FIREFIGHTER · Police ·
SUPPLIER · MOVER ·
Photographer · M·T ·
Dental · Medical
GEN WORKSHOP TECH ·
& MANY MORE
MODERN - Apprenticeships
EQUAL OPS
PVR
EDUCATION - Adventure Training
Regular & Reserve
NOT an Ordinary Job?
Royal AIR Force
TOTAL RAF Personnel
1918 - 291,170
2018 - 35,000 (APPROX) INC· RESERVES
GROUND TRADES EVOLVE
des

Youngsters suited to RAF Technical Trades?
"Hoover One" to "DAD Control"... the extension lead has reached it's limit TURN OFF POWER! I'M deploying RE-ENTRY Apparatus
CONTROL
DESMONDE

Youngsters suited to RAF NON technical Trades?
SPITFIRE
GLUE

On the Job Training.....
GOON MY SON MAKE as Proud just a bit louder with the SQUAWKING
NEWBIE
BIRD
CONTROL

I OLD Style Apprentices
"Trenchard Brats"
young, bright kids the RAF tech Vanguard
Many went onto great things but retain a nostalgic affection....
Psst do Me a favour you are now "seniorman" Keep an eye on this Lot & DON'T CRAP on the Floor I'll be back in a JIFFY!
... FOR GOATS, BAGPIPES & BRASSO!

Meet our New Dental Hygeinist he's ex RAF Regt.

"Workparty & "Janker Wallahs"
Somewhere in Germany a Secret Location...
OK boys we gotta tidy up we dont want people Hurting Themselves!
KEEP OUT DANGER
DANGER ARMED PATROLS

DON'T WORRY SIR NOBBY USED TO WORK ON THE FAIRGROUND

120

LEFT RIGHT
OPEN THEM LEGS
NUFFINKS GONNA
FALL OUT!

The Good News is you made Corporal
the Bad News is you gotta hand back the
Keyboard, the squeeze box & the Bugle....

The Central (One Man) Band of the RAF

Oh & by the way your being deployed to the
Middle East as a stretcher bearer... Sorry

The Bloodhound of Corporal Baskervilles

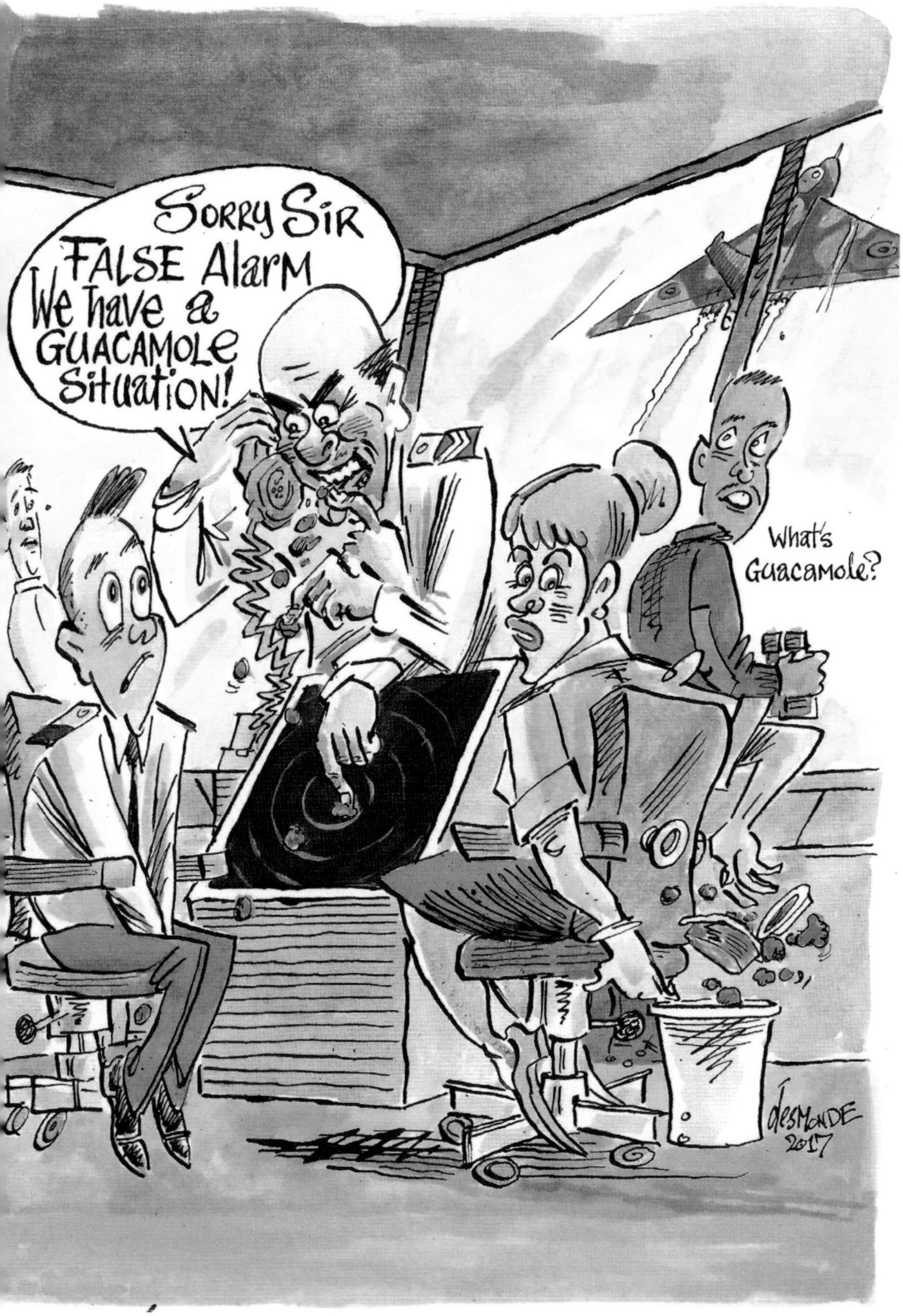
SORRY SIR FALSE Alarm We have a GUACAMOLE Situation!
What's Guacamole?
dESMONDE 2017

Aces High
Aces Low!
Beep!
Beep!

"Get Lost I'm Fine here if a Shell's got your Name on it..."
Armourer Humour
SAC TOM SMITH
desmonde 2018

The Arrival of the Long awaited GAffer TAPE!
DESMONDE 2017

My Dad says the
RAF Regiment Must
the only people in the
IR FORCE Who Can
operate an IRON!
Kid's NOT WRONG

Sibling Rivalry
Spoilt Brat Gets All the Best TOYS

Todays Forces are thinly spread & arguably Tri-Service Cooperation is more prevalent - As is the CHILDISH Inter Service Banter

CHEEKY Little Upstart
RAF COMING Through!
Make way Fella's
LOVE
HATE
DESMONDE 2018

I'M a great fan of equal opportunities but WHAT the ✡?X#!! is that PONGO doing here!
Equal Opportunities
desmonde

Tri-Service
NOSE ART
Royal Navy:
Golden Rings to pay for EMERGENCIES ie funerals, escort agencies etc
3
1
2
Army: Broken Nose Championship Heats
Colchester 'street' Boxing Awards
& the junior service....
Royal Air Force
the Aesthetic decoration of aeroplanes
DESMONDE

SOME Celebrated
BRIAN BLESSED (Actor) "The DRILL Corporal is IN SHOCK! he's Never heard a LOUDER VOICE than His OWN!"
PAM AYRES (Poet) "Do you know... There was an old Lady from EALING who had a peculiar feeling?"
Sorry Sir don't know that ONE!"
Audition
TONY HANCOCK (Comedian)
"Call that a PINT? It's Not even an ARM FULL!"
RALPH STEADMAN (Illustrator)
You Messy Little MAN
"I'm Working class I feel Inferior to him & him...."
Call that MARCHING you bunch of comedians
RONNIE CORBETT prior to being Commissioned. (Comedian & reluctant purveyor of Fork handles)
PETER SELLERS
FRANK MUIR

ex WRANKERS
BILL WYMAN (ROLLING STONE)
No Bill Forget about Music. Try Metal detecting
MINES
JOHN CHILTON (JAZZ MUSICIAN & author)
"hmmm very good you can be a Typist"
RAF Careers
DAVID BAILEY (Fashion Photographer)
"ere darling can I take your photo?"
DONALD McCULLUM (War photographer)
GRRRRR
OOOH
"ere guys can I take your photo?"
ARNOLD WESKER (Play writer)
What Chips with CUSTARD!
ERIC SYKES
DENNIS NORDEN
BOB MONKHOUSE
MAX BYGRAVES
desMONDE

More Celebrated

ex WRANKERS

PETER SALLIS (Actor)
You Got the WRONG TROUSERS!
JOHNY BALL (T.V. Presenter)
1,2,30,40,76,80 plus 40
Why did I tell him to NUMBER OFF!
JOHN NOAKES (T.V. Presenter)
DOWN SHEP
BRIAN CLOUGH (Footballer & Manager)
We don't have Berets BIG ENUFF FOR YOUR HEAD!
STORES
CAROL VORDERMAN (T.V. PRESENTER) Honorary Group Captain to AIR CADETS
Can We have a "P" Maam?
RODNEY BEWES (Actor) The Likely Lads
You're Brighter than your Mate Terry He joined the ARMY
DES O'CONNOR (Comedian)
Nah, Orange ain't down as an ethnic Origin!
DESMONDE

Let me see your ID's
RAF
K9's & 1250's!
Thanks to John Taylor (jailed) Al Macdonald &
Mark Dino for their stories of SHOWING I.D. to DOG!
DESMONDE 2018

Patient attempts to get out of Stretcher to help Medic who Tripped!
ooh let me help yoze Mate
Des Buckley 2016
Thanks to Laurence Rigby for the story

A helpful Officer....
I'LL JUST PLUG THIS LITTLE CHAP IN....
XR7 123
THANKS TO Lee 'Elsie' Edmonds for his story about his Dad: Ken Edmonds 1st "maiden flight"!
des

The Newbie asked to put tyre pressures on a Scorpion

CALL CONTROL. MISSION to DISPOSE of EXPLOSIVES SUCCESSFUL...BUT WE NEED a TOW BACK TO BASE...
Kaboom
2727
Thanks to Peter Baldock of 'CHABRO's Commandos' dedicated to Memory of Geordie NAYLOR!
DESMONDE 2018

ACCIDENT AND EMERGENCY
TAC-EVAL
BLUE ON BLUE BROKEN WRISTS THAT WAY
WARDS
TRIAGE
SNAP
THUD
A & E
THIS WAY JANET
DESMONDE 2018
THANKS to JANET McDIARMID for the Story RAF Exercises can be Bad for you!

Badly timed Wardrobe Malfunction...
HALF MAST AirWOMAN?
TELECOMS ADMIN
Thanks to Donna "Lumpy" Cook for story
DESMONDE 2018

TAKING ON a Spouses RANK

the Romantic Rockape Ambush
in Gas Testing Facility
HURRY UP SAY YES
Ahhhhhh Bless
Is she Crying or Blowing CHUNKS
I'LL MARRY HIM IF IT MEANS WE GET OUT

Fantastic Grouping
but so low...er...
Do I need to refer
you for Relationship
Counselling?
desmonde

Outa Bounds
CHALLENGE for determined Lovers
WRAF BLOCK

Why you seldom see Ground crew ghosts
GIT ORF MY GRASS YOU 'ORRIBLE LITTLE GHOULIES!
DESMONDE

YOU SEE THE RED ARROWS are gentlemen the BLOODY Groundcrew don't even REACH the TROUGH!

PROOF they Put BROMIDE in our Tea or URI Geller's joined up?
CLINK

When Wrankers ATTACK er... ...SNOW!
A BATTLE ACTION COMIC
No 74 1/-
SAY the WORD I'll BLAST IT!
WHERE DO YOU WANT the UREA?
OUR MISSION CLEAR the RUNWAY SO UNIVERSITY STUDENTS Can SCRAMBLE into their CHIPMUNKS...
HMMM NOT KEEN? OK...
RUM RATION
Note to Self DROP RUM FROM REGS IN 1980's
desmonde

CHEERS

This Impressionistic portrait of the 'Wrankers' is a modest attempt to shine a little bit of limelight on 100 years of service. This was more succinctly described by one of the UK's best loved writer and comedians.

Three Cheers for the man on the ground (1942) – abridged

He doesn't want glory, but please tell his story;
Spread a little of his fame around.
He's one of the few so give him his due;
Three cheers for the man on the ground.

*Acknowledgments to the estate and memory of former 'Erk' Eric Sykes

WRANKER CARTOON DIGIPRINTS

You may order digiprints of Cartoons by contacting me via my email address below. At the time of publication these cost £20 plus £7:50 for special delivery within the UK. I would be pleased to sign or add a personal message if required.

Should you require a copy of 'Women in the RAF 100' Cartoon contact me at the same email address and I will put you in contact with Trishia Welsh. Trisha commissioned the poster to raise funds and awareness of WINTRAF100.

There are no current plans to publish a follow up collection. Please 'like' my Wrankers Facebook page if you wish to be updated, which will feature occasional new cartoons.

enquiries@descartoons.co.uk

ACKNOWLEDGMENTS

A thin Cartoon module hardly warrants an appendix, however, I promised, to acknowledge the ex-Wrankers who sent in their stories. They are also credited on the original cartoon: Peter Baldock, Donna Cook, Janet McDiarmid, Brian Watling, Simon Parker, John Taylor, Al MacDonald, Mark Ding, Laurence Rigby, Katherine Griffiths, Lynne Stringer and Scott Mitchell. Regrettably some tales were unsuited to a single panel drawing. Others though hysterical were too toxic to publish. I used little from my short and inglorious RAF service for fear of provoking disbelief or betraying confidences. Many "Erk" tales seemed to be about jibbing authority, catastrophic incidents, injudicious drinking, affairs of the heart and getting one over superiors. This suggests just beneath the Erk's (brassoed' or Staybrite) tunic buttons there beats a truculent heart.

Laughable as it seems I carried out research & read dozens of books. For those curious about the Wranker experience I highly recommend the following.

- *From the ground up: a history of RAF ground crew* – F.J. Adkin
  Airlife Publishing Ltd 1983. ISBN 0 906393213
- *Wards in the sky (PMRAFNS)* – Mary Mackie
  The History Press 2001 and 2014. ISBN 978 0 7509 5956 8
- *Through adversity (RAF Regt.)* – Kingsley M. Oliver
  Forces & Corporate Publishing. ISBN 0 9529597 0 4
- *The Mint (1920s RAF Basic Training)* – T.E. Lawrence
  Tauris Parke Paperbacks (abridged). ISBN 978 1784535414

This may be out-of-print. Previous versions published by Penguin Modern Classics. Perhaps the most personal and revealing resource of all is the BBC's on-line People's War. Honest testimony from those who were there.

Thanks to Peter Cooke (Graphic Designer) for helping translate the bits of paper into PDFs and applying professional readable text to the covers.

With special acknowledgments to L/Cpl John 'J.P.' Buckley, ex Royal Fusiliers, A.C. Colin Chapman (AKA man with glasses) ex-RAF and Mr R.T. (The Quiet Man) R.I.P

Life's short, do it now…

Printed in Great
Britain
by Amazon

32367448R00056